# Ballet
## for a
# Funeral

## Scott Shaw

BUDDHA ROSE PUBLICATIONS

First Edition 2013

Library of Congress Control Number:
2013955985

ISBN-10: 1-877792-75-6
ISBN-13: 9781877792755

10 9 8 7 6 5 4 3 2 1

Printed in the United States of America

# Ballet for a Funeral

# contents

I was in this courtyard
that I had sat in
a million times before
drinking a nonfat latte'
and witnessing my life

my waffle
        with fresh strawberries
finds its way to the glass counter
the glass counter
in front of me
they call out my number

I get up/walk over
grab the whipped crème
spurt an ample amount
upon the top of the waffle
and sit back down

I'm eatin'
I'm drinkin'
when up walks this couple

white bread/wonder white bread

the chick looks at the menu
then she throws a fit
throws down the menu
and walks away
the dude chases after her

a few minutes later

I'm still eatin'
I'm still drinkin'
they come back
they sit down at the table
next to mine

the dude
begins
he goes into all this ass kissin' bullshit
tellin' the chick
that he's sorry
that it is just who he is
that he tries to help everyone/everything
the chick is sobbing
she cries in my left ear
fuck me!

the dude is sittin' there
apologizing/asking for forgiveness
...forgiveness from this ugly bitch

me, I wouldn't have even wasted my time

you know, I just don't get it
why play a bitch to a bitch
why ask for forgiveness
for just being who you are

I mean, tell the bitch,
*fuck you!*
*this is just who I am!*

you know, it is like
all the sports stars out there
who get caught
with their dick in some other pussy

and then they go all-beggin'
        back to their bitch
buyin' 'em diamond rings
houses/cars

I mean,
what the fuck did these bitches expect
when they got involved with a person like that

what?
that they were going to be
*happily-ever-after*
I mean come on!

and for this average dude
to kiss the ass of a very average bitch
who is sittin' there cryin'
cryin' in my ear
in public
I mean, come the fuck on!
it can only be down hill from there

so the bitch
continues to sob
the dude
continues to ask for forgiveness
me,
I couldn't take it anymore
I got up and left

all
poets/mystics/dreamers/artists
hope
that what they do
will be embraced

they think/believe
if not now
than at some later time
like van gogh/gauguin

but if not
what?
what does it all mean?
if not
why?
why did they live?
if all they created
all that they believed needed creating
meant nothing
then what?

what?
next to why?
the ultimate question

but the fact is
all art
is lost to the masses
once it is created
to all those who see it/read it
it doesn't mean
a god damned thing

the viewers
they're intellectuals
they see it/they read it
they think they know
but they never know
they don't know
they don't understand shit
they think they understand
but they don't
yet,
they pretend that they do

art/poetry/spirituality
it is lost
the moment it is created

      written down upon a page
      painted upon a canvas

      the vision
      it is actualized
      but its essence
      it is lost
            gone-gone-gone forever
            from the mind of the creator
            to those
            who can never
            truly understand its cause

that is art
...never understood

only believed
to be known

thus, art
thus, life
thus, the life of an artist
thus, their creations
       they mean nothing...

## three

I get drunk
every night

I sit back into the abyss
      of the abstract
and I drink
a bottle of wine

some call that alcoholism
I call it
a pathway to enlightenment
a necessary price
for a life/for a livelihood
where everything
means so little
where people strive and strive
and strive and strive
      and all they accomplish
      is things that add up to
      the meaninglessness
      of the nothingness of this world

maybe you don't understand
maybe you have not stepped
beyond the realms of the known/expected
existence
maybe
I cannot say

what I can say
is that when you know

you know
you know
that IT
IT
the ways/the promises
of the world
equal nothing
       so instead of buying into the lie
       I sit back
       and drink
       a glass of the grape

       a glass of the grape
       for all those who don't understand
       a glass of the grape
       for all those who don't see
       a glass of the grape
       for all those who partake of the lie
       that this
       will equal that
       that this
       will make you
       something more than nothing

       NOTHING
       the ultimate statement of zen

me
       I sit back
       and I have
       a glass of wine

14

## four

I got pissed off
at my woman
I took the glass in my hand
threw it at the wall

instead of hitting the wall
it hit the t.v.
broke
its thousand dollar screen

> the wine in the glass
> slapped its image
> upon the wall
> abstract art

goddamn it !!!

day next
I order a new t.v.
I had to pay for it
even though it was my woman
who had done something wrong

here
    is
    depicted
the
    essence
    of
    life

one of those
grey/overcast days in l.a.
the summer is coming on
so it is getting hot
that feeling
of uncomfortably hot
nasty hot

people are driving like shit
its friday
so they all have somewhere better to be
which makes them drive
        slower/badly/more dangerously

        they cut me off
        they stop for no reason
        I scream/I honk
        to no one's ears
        at least no one's ears
        that cares

this is the city
los angeles, california
city of cars/bars/stars
city of idiots

idiots
just like me

## six

I get an email from this kid in new york city
he's fourteen
he tells me I am one of his idols
tells me
      he wants to make a movie with me

      I smile
      I think back to fourteen
            fuck
            that was like forty something years ago
               ...seems like yesterday

I answer
play it cool/play it nice
      say, I'd love to
      but...
      it is just too involved
      to do a movie with me
      the rights/the releases
      he doesn't get it
      says, *thank you so much*
            for answering
            if I ever get my rights together
            let him know
      again I smile

today
I listened to a t. rex cd
listen in my car
I was fourteen when I saw him/them
play a concert
at the santa monica civic auditorium

that was
the summer before hollywood high school
I was there
I was duped up on acid
but I remember
marc bolan's fading glory
he was smashing a white les paul
near the end of the show
and nobody really cared
he had to yell,
*come on! get into it! this used to be one of my
favorite guitars!*
he died a few years after that
sadly...

but that was a long-long-long time ago

the dream(s) and life
and the idols that we all had
lost and gone
forever and ever

people like marc bolan
never even knew what an email was
just like me/just like you
      we are a fourteen year old dreamer
      then we are old
      then we are dead
      then all the newness that happens
      we never know anything about

there's this bar
over on the far west side
of san francisco
s.f. for the initiated

it is
down/dirty
like all bars should be
but it has some of the best
mac n' cheese
I have ever tasted
and believe me
       I'm a mac n' cheese connoisseur

I make my way inside its doors
every now and then when I'm up there

there's this
old grungy dude
he brings his dog in
wearing his doggy rain coat
...in the afternoons
I mean hey
it is s.f.
it rains a lot
he never eats the mac n' cheese
just throws back a brew or two from the tap
then he and his dog
they leave

the dog digs me though
most dogs do

animals
children
crazy people
and strippers
for some reason
they all seem to like me
why
I do not know

the people in the bar
they go and have their smokes
outside
> I mean hey
> this is the twenty-first century
> after all
> *no smoking inside*

me, I go in there
toss back a few *guinness*
eat a plate of the poison
and live life
in the dark
dingy
grimy wall of the place
it feels like home

there's a lot of chicks that go in there
but I've never scored any pussy
it is s.f.
most of the inhabitants
> are fags and dykes
> good for them
> not for me

I guess it's not politically correct
to say fags and dykes anymore
whatever...

anyway
I've never scored there
but there have been a few
of the female species
who have set my juices flowin'
cast my mind to fantasy
maybe someday...
but just not today

so
like all lost poets/dreamers
I sit back
eat some great mac n' cheese
toss back a few dark ones
and relish the moment(s)
as they slowly drift away
towards oblivion

## eight

I walked out of the door of my apartment
     this afternoon
moving in the direction of my car
I see the building manager
she said,
*hi. we've got to stop meeting like this.*
     we smile
     we talk
     we say nothing

I ask,
*how long have you been here now; a year?*
*oh no, two and a half*
*wow, times flies...*

I get in my car
I leave
I drive to starbucks
one of the workers gets in line behind me
I insist
she move in front
     we smile
     we talk
     we say nothing

*how long have you been here now,* I ask
*three months?*
*no, only one...*

     how times flies
     in the opposite direction

22

I go out
I do what I do
I'm driving home
I listen to the radio
one of those
            public radio international programs

a guy
he tells a story
he speaks of getting old
of meeting a woman on the internet
they inter-act
on-line
they finally decide to meet
meet
            face-to-face
she is all he had ever hoped for
she sees him
            he is far too old
            he walks with a cane
time/life had passed
the chance is gone

it happens to all of us

        how times flies...

on the road
sedona to l.a.
stop for gas
blythe

pay the lady
pump the gas
get my change
head for the head
      men's room
      it said so...

I reach
I open the door
it was unlocked

there sitting
      doing her business
a lady
long wavy black hair
      pretty
her thighs
nude
etching her form
as she sits

for that second my gaze is locked
for that moment her gaze is locked

then
*I'm sorry,* she exlcaims
I close the door

I leave the establishment
I get in my car
I drive off
go to hit the head at starbucks

one of those moments
lost/locked to eternity
here on this page
embarrassment
lust
all cast to the realms
of life/of desire
of all the juices that are/were stirred
by our very brief meeting

I will never see her again
not her face
not her eyes
not her long flowing hair
not her naked thighs

that's sad, I think
I would have liked to have known
her/them
more

there is a lot of negativity
surrounding my world

I look down
out/over
the midnight ocean
off in the distance
it is so-so-so far away

far away
not like the old days
not like
in the old days
not like when life mattered

I was there/right there
on her
listening to every wave

now
ten years deep
here I sit
in the midnight sun
and I see her
see the moon caressing her
but she
is so-so-so far away

I sit out on my patio
a glass of the grape in my hand
I listen

I am forced to listen
hear
the conversations/the arguments
the words of my neighbors

some are in farsi
some in korean and chinese
some even in english

all are spoken in/of un-peace

*fuck you! fuck you, bitch!*
*you white trash bitch!*
*I will bounce if you just give me my bags!*

my lady
she is asleep
she questioned
before she went to slept
*is it the full moon?*
*maybe that's why*
*everybody is fighting*

but, no
no, it is not the full moon
it is just another day
that has turned into another night
where I am living
where I don't want to live
surround by the masses
who hold no vision

those who hold/embrace
only desire
only anger
only frustration

me
I have killed another bottle
another bottle of the grape

what does that make it?
number fifteen million and thirty-five
...or something like that

drinking
trying to hide
drinking
trying to maintain
drinking
trying to live in a world
where I am surround by the angry
the frustrated
the vision-less

me
I am forced to listen to them
instead of the waves
instead of the divine mother ocean
me
I am trying to remain me
but time
but life
but pursuing the dream
it has taken its toll

w/no money/no real/BIG money
to get back
to where I need to be
next to her/the ocean
so, I am lost
I sit here on my patio

I stare off at the ocean
in the distance
and I listen to those
who fill the night air with anger
I listen to those
destroying their lives
taking my life/my moment(s)
away from me
me, as I try to remain
holding onto/living the dream
w/ no finances
to do so

thus
I am cast to the world/a world
surround by anger/dominated by hate

as they speak
as they scream
I sit down
w/ another bottle done
and only the dream
to get back
to where I once was
to where I belong

## eleven

I sit back into the oblivion
I look out there
into the distance
across the living room
there sits
a pikachu
there's a hello kitty on the bookshelf
via china
dressed in traditional chinese garb
a buddha lamp
a female buddha

me
today
first I was in san francisco
the rain was raining
then/now
I'm in l.a.
lost in my abode

I have a pure white persian cat
she walks right up to me
she has blue eyes
like mine

she wants love
she wants something/anything

I get up from the couch
she follows
she speaks
saying something

something
what?
I do not know

I walk
she follows

today
earlier
san francisco
there she was
this divine asian form of a female
she had a slit
up the side of her skirt
and
if you looked closely/quickly
just for a moment
you could see
she had nothing on underneath
there it was
the perfect vision
the perfect source of life
giving
everyman/everything
something worth living for
but then she was gone
nothing/nada

as I drove down the coast
s.f. to l.a.
I stopped
I step into a starbucks
catch a latte' for the road

again/another
perfect form
of abstract female perfection
she turns around
from the line that formed in front of me
she looks me up and down
studies me
very-obviously
she asks me
who makes the suit you're wearing
*armani*
I answer
she says,
*you look like you deserve to wear amani*

what the fuck does that mean?

but I didn't ask
couldn't pursue the question
couldn't purse her
I wasn't alone
my lady she waited in the car

and what does it all mean
what could it all be
all it is/all it was

*fuck me,* I thought
I have been making this drive
for thirty/no forty
years now
but still here I am
stitched in the lust

lost in the wonderment
adrift
driving from s.f. to l.a
l.a to s.f.

11:01 pm
I arrive home
having driven that course
one million times or more

I look at the moment(s)
I think of the hour(s)
hour(s) of life spent
lost on the road
lost lusting for the dream

lost
in the/this world
of where any dream will do

I crack a bottle of the grape
I sit back
my lady
she went to bed

my other persian cat
orange/white
sits, then lays
down next to me
I take a sip
as my cat purrs

I drink to the world of wonderment
the world of, *what if*

san francisco
just there
l.a.
too late

my life
too long
too dreamed
a dream unlived
should never be
a dream forgotten

I write these words
I drink this wine
I sit
and look at my space
and I wonder...
I wonder, *why*

another little hottie
knocks my socks off
sweet young latina
long
flowing
black
hair
she wears a scarf
to keep it in place
perfection in the making
love for the taking

she glances my direction
likes what she sees
smiles
small talks

do I want her?
fuck yeah

do I desire here?
you know it

but here is the question
what am I?
fifty-five
what is she?
maybe twenty
maybe younger

my mind goes to all the things
I would love to do to her

how I would l like to touch her body
how I would like her to touch mine
I would do what I always do
love her like she's never been loved
love her like she will never be again
I am a master/I am a pro
at the game of love

she obviously likes what she sees
which makes it/this all the worse

could it/can it happen
yeah, it looks that way
but then what
what do I/would I have
to offer her
just another momentary fix
from a life lived too long
just another momentary promise
like all the one's before
another promise
I could not/can not keep
so I sit here
lost in the question
questioning the dream
have her/take her
make her love me
like I have done
so many times before
and then what
all I would have to leave her with
is another ruined young girl's life
I have ruined so many/too many

## thirteen

I have been around the world
what is it?
seventeen times
or something like that
I have been
halfway here/halfway there
more time than I can
count/remember
I've seen things/I've done things
that most people
would not/could not
even believe

I've gone
I've done
I've seen
I've conquered
and still
here I am
much longer than I
ever thought I would/should be

and what am I left with?
enlightenment?
that's easy

money?
spend it all

experience?
yeah, whatever...

it's all the chase of all the dreams
that's what has kept it going
the promise of what's not/is not
and what is promised
that can never be

so, to be me
no
it wasn't that great
in fact it was very-very-very hard

I jumped onto the bandwagon
of artistic belief
trusted that art would equal something
but it does not
art only equals art
good or bad
that's all it is
art only equals
the promise of further illusion
the hope that someday
it will all mean something
but it does not
art only equals
trying to figure out
how you are going to pay your rent
how you are going to buy the things
you want/you need
how you are going to live
when you are all-alone
all this
while others dwell in the world
of the real/of the accepted

but me
I sit in the gaping/griping realms
of the abyss of abstraction

trying to find a way
to live the next dream
it is/my life was/is
very-very-very hard

a street
over looking the ocean
the waves crash down
below my feet

a lady pulls up in her car
she gets out
she lets her kid out

he walks in the direction of the sea
he stands on the same small wall
that I stand on
a smile comes over his face
he is embraced
he is enthralled
he is lost in the substance
the essence
of the divine mother ocean
he/just like me

no other place I should be
no other place I want to be
but by her
listening to her/absorbing her
divine perfection
divine meditation
divine emancipation
I am where I should be
as is the boy

the mother/she...
she is just on a play date

taking the kid/her kid
somewhere
someplace to keep him occupied

but me/but him
I see it in his eyes
the smile in his eyes
he understands
the subtle realms of wisdom
the abstract realms of enlightenment
he knows
she/his mother
does not

the mother grabs the beach bag
she takes hold of her son's hand
they walk down the stairs
in the direction of the water
closer
to the essence of perfection
his smile remains

me
I stand there distant
I stand there in the distance
standing on a small wall
that boarders the sidewalk
framed by the street

I stand there
lost in the looking
listening to the sound

my mind wanders
my mind is lost
my mind is enthralled

I think back to when I was as a child
me/just like him
just like that little boy
even then I knew
knew/like him
felt/understood
the divine perfection of the sea
of she
where I always should be
here I always am

me and she
her and I
the divine mother ocean
it is part of me/full in me
what I am
who I am
forever
as long as I am

the moon bleeds its essence
out over the ocean
the light moves light
etching the western sky

so many years have I seen her
so may years have I stared
into her depths
the ocean
no one could love her
more than I

today
this day
I spend a day writing/transcribing
poems
from twenty-five years ago
putting them to type
keeping them
from being lost/forgotten

tonight
I watch a new midnight talk show
with a talk show guy
from twenty-five years in the past
he's back/he flashes back
to scenes lived long ago

he/they
his guest
they were much younger then
me too
me too

and now
here I sit
a glass of grape in my hand
watching flashbacks
from t.v. twenty-five years deep
after reading words
penned twenty-five years ago
the coincidence can-not be overlooked

poetry
t.v.
and me
still here I sit
staring into the abyss of the night
the depths of the midnight sea
remembering what was
dreaming of what is to come
as the moon
lights/illuminates
the ocean
and I think back
to times past
with a glass of wine in my hand

a day lays out in front of me
distant
grey
unusually uncool
for the end of july

a day
like all the others
people walk
people drive
people go to work

me, I am free
free
w/ out the finances
to be truly free

free
but nowhere to go/nothing to do

free
lost in the abyss

## seventeen

I think
most people
cannot even comprehend
how many days/nights
of my life
I have simply asked for death

what are there
three-hundred sixty-five days in a year

three-hundred sixty-five days a year
in that time frame
I have probably drank three-hundred
and eighty bottles of wine
a few hundred beers

hard alcohol
rarely touch it
there's just no mysticism
gained in those realms

life/death
dreams/lived
desires/lost & fulfilled
you just don't know what it's like
to live my life
an artists life
you just don't know...

you see
here's the deal
if you're not slammin' down
a bottle a night
a bottle a night
for ten
fifteen
twenty years
then you just
don't get it
you do not understand

and I say that
AGAIN

if you're not slammin' down
a bottle a night
a bottle a night
for ten
fifteen
twenty years
then
YOU DO NOT UNDERSTAND

for out there
on the outskirts
out there
where the dreams happen
out there
where the dreams are real
where any dream will do

where only the dreamers know/understand
true reality
then
THIS IS IT

IT

the moment/the life
the only/the all

the only place where you can find the truth
in the words/in the writings
of the mystics

everybody speaks
most should shut the fuck up
they don't know shit
yet, still the talk
as if they do

they haven't lived
no, they haven't live
no, not really
no, not true reality

for out here on the outskirts
out here
where the dreams happen
out here where the dreams are real
a crossing over of consciousness
from ethereal to real

only here
does the essence of existence
truly take hold

THIS IS IT

IT

the moment
the life
the only
where you
-the only-
find the truth in the words
of the mystics
and transcend the writings
of the fools

THIS IS IT

IT

the mystic/the artistic
the passageway
where we dwell in hell

this is it
this is what you seek
the realm(s) of
the dwellers/the realizers
of the art

seek
but you cannot find
have
have it all

the all/the nothing
they hype/the fear
the dream of the dreaming
the longing...

so drink
drink into the late night
drink
all alone
all invasive/all pervasive
ALL

all the all
the all of nothing

you want to know the art
than achieve nothingness
no-thing-ness

all the hype
all the dreams
all the desires
but this is it
this is all there is
the end of days
the end of the all
the end of the illusion

no-thing-ness
zero
this is art
this is what you achieve from art
...from living the life of an artist

welcome to my world

the world of the artist
the world of the daydreamer
the world of the mystic
the world of the drunk

enter
if you dare
buy beware
there is no way out

l.a.
always a multi-ethnic place

multi-ethnic...
that sounds so twenty-first century
so politically correct
...I smile

but l.a
there was never a time
when I was not surrounded
by every race/every color
lost languages
spilling their way
into my ears
as far back
as I can remember
through every memory/thought/placement
of said/and as such
it was never not there

me
a beachside cafe
language(s) drift into my ears
they cross mingle
I hear
I understand some
others I do not
I do not listen
I do-not/I can-not
care

care about what those people care about
I just cannot bring myself to do so

l.a.
here I am

a 1964 song from the beatles
plays in my ears
I hear it
from a car
that pulls up to the stop light
that
I would listen to
that
I could care about

me
I sit here
a beachside cafe
bordering the ocean
as john lennon sings in my ear
singing in english
the only english
that I hear

the light changes
red to green
the car, with the music, drives off
john lennon sings no more

a cement mixer truck
drives by

a meter maid cart
with her lights flashing

is next to pass

a red jeep
drives its way
between me and the sea

I sit here
at the ocean
l.a.
and I hear people speaking
but I hear no english

strange…

but this is l.a.

listening
old people/old ladies
talk

they discuss
their reality
how they see pop culture
what they think
about donnie and marie
their words...
*I found out they are back as a team*
*doing what they do*

they talk
about adoption
they question
*if a person is adopted*
*will they still possess the addictive personality of*
*their biological parents*

we all talk
we all discuss the bullshit
of our lives
the bullshit
that means nothing to no-body else

god
I hope I never get old
old/too old
to have no understanding
of the life and the time(s)
existing in a current moment
of my history

driving drunk
midday
late summer
afternoon

hot/sunny

people sit on a bus bench
lost
in the sun

a lady
blonde
probably an ex-hippie
trying to save the earth
but by doing so
she is being crucified by he sun

she sits on the bench
next to a black man
a black man who sits next to his little girl
maybe three years old
he holds her hand

he's old though
too old
too old to be having a kid that young
old/grey/wrinkled

she
the three year old
sits and cries

it's too hot/too sunny
to be sitting on a bus bench
midday

but there they are
lost/left for dead
while pretending to be alive

three of them
there
with no way in/no way out

this is the city
los angeles, california

it's all about the long haul
those
who do not give up
when the dream(s) gets deep

do you know
how many of my party buds
have quit
though I thought they never would
...thought they would never die
...believed
they would never
give up the dream

the dream of the illusion
lived by those of us
out here on the streets
...the late night streets
out here in the depths
of living fantasy
longing lust
in the realms
of the never-never

but they all did
they're all gone
gone to the dark abyss
of the meaningless
of the average
of the nothing

so this is for the few of us
who still dwell at the gates of hell

those of us who find our enlightenment
in the drink
in the life
lived on the edge

lived on the edge
w/ those
who no one else wants
no one else can accept
no one else can understand

so the kiss goes on
forever and ever and ever
the kiss of the drink
it is such a cheap kiss
to buy
while the illusion
dances on our souls
w/ lust pretending to be love
cheap women = cheap illusion

and from this/that
where the knowledge/the realization
is born
this is for the few of us who remain
who understand
that our enlightenment
will never be lost
to the life of the mindlessness masses

as
we
have
truly
lived
what others

the unenlightened
can never understand

so I give a kiss goodnight
to all those who have fallen
from the path/fallen from the fray
a kiss goodnight
to all the women
I have spent moments with
yet I can't for the life of me
remember your names

a kiss goodnight
as I raise another glass
to my lips
and taste the sweet nectar
of the grape

psycho bitch
a step in front of me
at starbucks

you can feel them
how they breath/how they breed
danger
in the making
love
for the taking

all dudes
dig 'em
the psycho bitch
there is a lust
that they permeate
a desire
for devastation

I have lived their reality
one too many times

hot
they breathe hot promised passion
in a world that they will destroy
destruction
the ultimate evolution
passion
the ultimate lie

...she
she turns around in the line and looks at me

...she
she has found her prey
...she
she knows what she wants
believes I have stepped into her web

*fuck me*
I say to myself
*here it comes again*

...me
I get my latte'
non-fat, of course
I get my whole-wheat bagel
I go outside
to sit in the shade
of the patio

...she
she finds her way outside
...she
sits down near me
just then
her phone rings
she answers

it's her recent ex...
very recent
last night
I could not help but hear her conversation
as it took place

right next
to my left ear

...she

she speaks to her ex
it is revealed
he called the cops on her last night
he called them
but he wants her back
wants to give it/her/them
another go

their conversation goes
on and on and on and on
it echoes in my ear(s)

this
when all I want(ed) to do is eat my bagel
drink my latte'
and in the betterment of an even better world
perhaps fuck her
quick/easy
hit it/forget it
but no...
I have to listen to her discussion
the discussion of a psycho bitch
and her details of all of the reason(s)
I must run away

they talk
I cannot help but listen

*once the cops are called*
*i'm done*
so she states

...me
I love it
she obviously flipped out
did something supremely wrong

he called the cops
to chill it/her/the situation down
but
like only a psycho bitch would/could do
she blames him for the inevitable

I don't know...
maybe she thought this would impress me
maybe she thought I needed to hear
that she was free/ready to move on
I don't know...
she said it/so I could here it
she spoke it/so it would be heard
I don't know...
...because you never know
what a psycho bitch has on their mind

but
as she said to him/her very recent ex
*that was the first straw of the last straw*

profound dialogue
I thought

*first straw of the last straw*

...she
she finished her conversation
closed her phone
looked over at me and smiled
I didn't return the glance

with my bagel finished
I got up and left

it's been too many times deep
to knowingly fall back into
*the world of the psycho bitch*

though they always seem to be hot/pretty/sexy
always get your dick hard
and always promise illusion

...me
I just don't need it/all that
no
not
anymore

## twenty-four

I went through my library today
it had gotten
very-very-very-very big

I went through it today
to clear out the excess weight

texts I didn't want
text I couldn't sell
it took me most of the day

that/it/the process of
made me think back
back to back when...
back when I had an even bigger
massive-massive-massive-massive
library

but back then
it was a different group of books
it was made of texts I wanted to read
satchidananda
sivananda
reps
watts
leary
ram dass
rajneesh
khan (father & son)
kerouac
yogananda
bukowski
morrission (jim)

smith (patti)
hari dass (baba)

that was me
that was who I am/what I was
those books filled my consciousness

then came the early 1990s
I hit some financial hard times
it happens to the best of us
so I sold it all
all my
massive-massive-massive-massive
library

in a way it was freeing
books weigh a lot...

then somewhere in the late 1990s
I came to a realization
the understanding
I knew a lot about books

with this
and with the every-emerging
dawning and expansion of the internet
I had a realization
I could buy and sell books
make a little money on the side
this I did/this I do

but with this/and with that
there builds up a lot of books
a lot of books that I
just don't care about
and a collection of books

that
for whatever reason
do not sell

so there they sit
sit, on the bookshelves
until a cleansing takes place
I did that today

as I did
I realized as I looked at all the books
that inhabit my life
few of them I would even open the pages of

like life
this is it
we do what we do to make a living
to pay our bills
we do what we do
but does it do us?
and from it
sometimes we become so burdened
that we just have to clean house
cleansed
I am lightened
hey mr. palos verdes public library
a big donation is coming your way

there's this guy I know
put him in one of my movies
a couple of years ago
good dude

told today is his birthday
told he has developed cataracts
told he was supposed to re-take his driving test
told it was due a year ago
told he can't take it
'cause he can't pass the eyes test
told he still drives his truck
I smile
shake my head
in disbelief

here's a guy
seventy-fours years deep in life
bad eyesight
and driving

just yesterday
I saw an asian lady
laying bloody on the street
a car getting on the freeway
didn't see her
hit her

the ambulance was there
as was her bleeding face and head
unseen
can be deadly

can't see
can be even deadlier

no one wants to get old
but old we all get
...if we live that long
no one wants to stop doing
what they want to do
but time is an evil master
it takes from us all

what can you do
in the what can you do department?
nothing
this is just how life is
people do what they do what they do
do it
until maybe they kill someone

an asian lady
walking in a crosswalk
by the on ramp to the freeway

eatin' at a place I've eaten at for thirty years
over by the beach
I've seen the staff
come and go
but some are still there
there
...all this time
scary !!!

this waitress
or should I call her, *a server*
I think that's what they want to be called now
I don't know
it all gets kind of weird
what's the right word/the proper term
of the/this moment
and the moment(s)
they always change

anyway...
known her a couple of three years now
she comes up to take my order
the *how's it going(s)*
go around

in response
her
she's none too happy
her roomie is moving out
needs someone else to move in
I suggest she should get a man

*that's exactly what I'm thinking*
she exclaims
*I have one in mind*

*oh really. that's great*
I state
*do I know him?*
coyly she points at me under her writing pad

awh god
fuck me
here I go again
what am I supposed to do with this
I must be two decades older than her
though that certainly would not/does not
stop me from tapping that ass
but I just don't need another woman
who needs
I've put a couple through college
one through grad school
spent fortunes that equaled nothing
not that she/this server
is not pretty
not that I would not have
meaningless sex
with her in a heartbeat
but I just don't need another
go-no-where
into the oblivion of life
meaningless relationship
that all I come away with
is lost time in a life
that has so few days left

love
when you are young
it promises everything
live a few years
believe me
you will not think that way
no, not any-more

dreams
on a cloudy rainy day
l.a.
home
and the essence lives
in the promise of illusion
a new girl/a new dream
has found her way to me

once
I took them all/accepted them all
didn't care the cause or the causation
now
I must think
time/age
so much more to lose

she is sweet
asia
a little cubby
cubby in just the right way
she holds a dream
not a dream of me
no
not like those dreams
that some have held in the past
no
a dream of the dream
she has her own dream
has a life that she feels is worth living

god
I find that refreshing

so the promises are in the wind
the promises of the illusion
held by the wind
I need say nothing
but live everything

a meet leads to a kiss
a kiss to a removal
of the tides that bind
and we find ourselves
lost/locked
in the passion

I like passion
it reveals a lot

and the kiss is lived
and the cause forgotten
all we have is each other
in this time/in the space
and the each other is all we need
she knows it
I pretend that I do
but it/this/us
locked in the realms
of the haveable
reveals all

will it last till tomorrow
I don't really care
for here
for now
we have all we need

sitting in a courtyard
a latte' in my hand
the sound of the street
pounds in my ears
I can see
the cars
the trucks
the motorcycles
the busses
pass by
through a hedge of plants
designed to do just that
divide us/me
from the sites and sounds
of the city
it only partially works

the day
here in so cal
cool and sunny
but the sun is
right now
hidden by a cloud
that's aok w/ me

me, I am protected
protected by a green umbrella
placed in the courtyard
next to the table
where I sit
placed here
by those who run/operate
this establishment

coffee
a courtyard
outside
as the city pounds
I have lived this scene
a million times
and perhaps
if I live long enough
I will live it
a million more

I don't know...

ocean in front of me
pacific
it sings in my right ear

two dudes next to me
speaking russian
that fills my left ear

two chicks
speaking japanese
I hear them somewhere in the distance

the sky is grey
it is late spring
I look out onto the horizon
the grey sky merges
with the grey of the ocean
somewhere
off/lost
there
in the
surreal distance

this is l.a.
this is life
my life
I put my feet up
lean back
and live it

last time
for a long time

a little
not too ugly
red headed
former crack ho'
of a coffee shop hostess

yeah
she used to come up
and talk and talk and talk to me
in other words
she was interested

I wasn't

she was young/I was old
she wanted to call me
I didn't want her to

I mean
where could it have lead

so I sit here
same restaurant
years later
and I remember her
I remember to remember
remember
the memory
of a time
a long time ago

*all my friends are dead*
I state
*what about me?*
climes in my buddy
*except you*
laughingly I exclaim

we had been talking
he had brought up the names
of several of our long time known(s)
who were currently succumbing
to the hands of fate/close to meeting
mr. death

I think back/we think back
to all those
we had known
who had already past
...the list is long

it reminds me of the song
jim carroll sang
*all my friends that died-died*
*they were all my friends*
*and they died*
jim carroll
now
is also dead

people come/people go
we live/we die
some last longer than others
some not

why/who
no one will ever know
but
time has past
lives have past
from my earliest memories forward
I have witnessed it
gone
so many are gone

gone
like the chant from the *Heart Sutra*
*gate' gate' pargate'*
*parsom gate'*
*bodhi swaha*

gone gone
gone beyond
gone beyond beyond to the great awakening

some people want to believe in the after-life
they want to believe
they can spend eternity
with the one(s) they love
but if you think about it
that is pretty stupid/very simplistic
for what is this realm of desire
but simply that
a realm of desire
love is a desire
lust is a desire
desiring forever is a desire

how can desire
transcend this limited plane of existence?

some people hold onto
the theory of reincarnation
they want to come back
again and again and again and again
a foolish concept
how can the I/the YOU
be more than what YOU are here/now
why would it/YOU travel
through space and through time

ego
wants to believe
the I will live on forever
but it cannot/will not

so what is there?
there is nothing
there is this moment
of self-consciousness
then it is gone
we are only remembered
by the one(s) who knew us
by the one(s) who thought they knew us
by the one(s) who wanted to know is

but known is gone
when this life is gone
it is gone
gone is gone
they all are gone

a *native-american/american-indian*
or whatever is proper to refer to
those of that descent
he was a guy
smoking
in a non-smoking place
more and more of the world
has become non-smoking
and that's good
smoking is a nasty habit

anyway
he lit up
I got up
just don't want to smell/breathe
that shit

looking at him
I could tell
his life had been hard
life on the res

most people
don't know it
few know of it
yeah, we all feel sorry for what
the *white-man* did
but few people take the time
to realize
it is still going on

life on the res
is very hard

it breeds a hard breed
that live
but never can truly live
trapped by what society has become
trapped by how
their world/their reality/their culture
was robbed from them

yes
it still goes on

I know this guy
he hails from gallop, new mexico
he still speaks/remembers/remarks
how *native-americans*
would drink/get drunk/pass out
and in some case die
freeze to death
in the night

*we called them popsicles*
he exclaimed

how cruel a comment/how unthinking a fate

a people
lost in a time/space/reality
not of their creation
with no way back/no way home
yet they try to live
fight their way to freedom
be
where it is so hard to be
some have made it
I know a few
many have not

as there is no way to fight
what you cannot see

this guy
the guy I write of
I could see in that guy's eyes
he was one of them
one of the broken/damaged/destroyed

he lit up
in a no-smoking zone
me
I let him have his moment/his space
I left

everybody is fucked up

sometimes at night
I like to take a walk
get the blood flowing
a time to reflect
about the goings-on
of the day/of life

I have these neighbors
really-really pretty people
she
she's blonde
about as pretty as a blonde girl can get
he
he's half asian
wears a ponytail
works outs
big muscles

though she seems to be a bit of
an agoraphobe
...stays home a lot
but you can't fault her for that
the world
out there
does suck
sucks
on the serious side

but and in the any case of
I was taking a walk

the other evening
with my lady

as we pass by their
place/space
she
the pretty blonde girl
plainly exclaims
*please don't hit me*

now any person of any mind
would wonder
how a guy
could hit a girl
as pretty as her
some may even question
how a guy
could hit any girl
of and for
but I won't go into all that
at least not here

I guess he didn't hit her
didn't hear a smack
nor a scream
but it is obvious
what goes on behind
their walls of fate

once
awhile back
in the same place/space
before they moved in

they
the couple I am discussing
there lived another couple
same place/same space

now that guy
and his chick
nowhere near as pretty
but they used to fight
he used to smack her up
one time
after one such incidence
as I was walking by in the night
I heard her say
*I'm sorry baby for disrespecting you*
meaning
she felt she deserved it

I joking told my lady
*see, that's how a woman is supposed to behave*

but life
it is complicated
people are never who they seem to be
the inside
hides from the outside
and you can never know what goes on
on
on the inside
from the outside

maybe it is that place/space
that attracts that kind of couple

maybe it is that place/space
that breeds that type of
inner-couple violence

I don't know
I will never know
we/us/you/me
can never know
we can not see
the inside
from the outside

but for whatever the cause and purpose
the karma and the destiny
I do know this
everybody is fucked up

## thirty-four

I look up to the sky
stare at a cloud
stare into space
the space of the spaced
I look up
and remember
remember
staring at a cloud
maybe thirty years ago
a cloud
pagan, burma
now myanmar
I remember
being out there in the distance
deep in the lost
realms of asia
out there
where illusion means something
out there
where living the dream(s)
are just a moment away

I remember
as I sit here in the city
l.a.

me
I feel damned
damned
like so many other dreamers
needing money to survive
life it is so wrong

the dreamers
the artists
the mystics
of which I am all three
they should have their way paved for them
a road
not of the masses
but of the few
given to/taken care of
but no
life/this world
it is not that way

so me
I sit here
minutes until call-time
waiting/hating
sitting in the cool
afternoon sun
waiting for my job to begin
where I go spit out
a few pre-written lines
and pretend to be
someone I am not

I look to a cloud
I remember...

*you want to get in my pants*
*don't you*
so says a sweet little hot chocolate mama
*well, only if you want me in them*
so I reply
*I do. I do*
*but you gotta know its good*
*probably the best you'll ever have*
*and after you taste it*
*you won't want to go away*

we met
her and I
at a store
she was shopping for a coffee pot
she asked me what I thought
I told her
one thing leads to another
you know how it goes

her pants
jeans
ass tucked tightly into them
not really the style I like
me, I am
and have always been
into the more classic
long flowing skirts
sort of thing

but she
she had an image

a look
that promised something other
than what was seen on the outside
so I took the chance

*with every dance there is another chance*

so we did what we did that afternoon
and as I have long realized
the minute a woman says she is the best
she is not

what makes them think that?
I don't not know
it just was what it was what it was

so I cast that/it/her/the experience
to these words of remembrance
remembrance for a moment
that was nothing more than just that

a kiss hello
always equals a kiss goodbye
the only defining factor is
how long it takes
between the two

she was probably pretty
when she was young
but she obviously allowed herself
to become
nothing more than average

life and time
and who we are

life and time
and what the world makes us

life and time
and desire(s) fading fast

life and time
and we forget our dreams

we allow ourselves to be forgotten
we forget who we are

who we are and what we are
created in our mind
projected in our life

it is all the illusion
but life is an illusion
so we have to play the game

she was probably pretty
once
but she obviously allowed herself

to become
nothing more than average

who have I/who have you
allowed
ourselves to become

*thirty-seven*

walked past a coffeehouse today
one that I first went into
maybe twenty-five years ago
back when it first opened

back then...
the first wave of the new wave
of coffeehouses
before starbucks took over the world

it was a different time
then...
the cool/the in the know/movie stars/rock stars
were the only ones in there

now it has all changed
now...
inhibited by the dirty
those who look like they
seriously need a bath
and a laundromat
they sit there
there in the widow
on beverly blvd.
pretending to write their scripts
hell, maybe they actually are
writing a screenplay
who cares!
it is a script no one will ever read
or see on the silver screen

yeah,
life was different back then

me...
I even held a few
meet and greet casting sessions
inside its doors
it was safe/common/abstract/free
free
except for the coffee
of course

I even met a sweet young lady
through those sessions
one I spent a moment in time with

time
like experience
like ambiance
it always moves on
on and on
moves onto the now

now...
now it is all different
the world is different
screenwriters dreaming of the dream
they sit at every coffeehouse/every starbucks
pretending to be writing something
something that has meaning
something that will launch their dreams

their dream
not yours or mine
dirty...
they always look so dirty

but that's just life
that's just time
everything changes
even when the structures are still the same
the businesses still business-ing

what was
comes and then it is gone
who was
is there no longer
like life
it all changes
we all get old
we all die
and then
it/the everything
is all gone

goodbye to the once was
I remember you/I miss you

*thirty-eight*

I have this idiot
who moved in next-door to me
he talks and talks and talks and talks
he obviously likes the sound of his own voice
loudly
very loudly
constantly
he's on the phone
he speaks
about all this new age bullshit
fancies himself
some kind of guru
he gives advice
tells people lies
borrow all his words
from what has been written
a thousand times before
but just like the authors
who could actually lay claim to the words
it is all bullshit
it is all lies
it is all promises
for a life
that could/can never be
experienced

when he is not preaching
I can hear him stomping on the floor
and screaming
*fuck me, fuck me, fuck me and mine*
like a dark mantra
he recites it over and over and over again

but the people he speaks with
never hear/never know this
they think/believe he has something
worth saying
he does not

just like all the want-be gurus
all the self-proclaimed spiritual teachers
they are all full of shit
trying to be/pretending to be
something that they are not

but me
like being cursed by the damned
paying for someone else's karma
I am forced to listen
to it/to him

this is not the first time
this has happened to me
not the first time
I have lived this experience

back when I used to live in hermosa
probably twenty-five/thirty years deep now
there was this guy that moved in
upstairs from me
me
in my beach apartment

he told everyone to just call him, *monk*
as we probably couldn't pronounce his name

I laughed in his face
laughed, back then...

me, who had been walking
the spiritual path forever
me, who had been all across asia
lived there
me, who spoke fluent sanskrit
well at least I did back then

he was a white guy like this guy
this guy my neighbor
white hair/white beard
like this guy
this guy my neighbor

didn't hear him speak a lot
that guy/back then
but had to listen
as he pounded his way up the stairs
all hours of the day and the night
women/men in tow
if you understand
what I am referring too

this
though he initially claimed
he needed quite
as he meditated a lot
but like all those who claim spirituality
it was all just bullshit
finally
I couldn't take it
no, not anymore

me, I moved out
like I would do now
if only
I had the/any money

I do not
...moving is expensive
if I had the/any money
I would move
but money
I have none
so I am damned/cursed/karma-ed
forced to listen to all the new age bullshit
that I have spend my entire life
running away from

my advice
think who you are listening to
before you start
listening to them

old...
...age happens

I sit
where I have sat
a million times before
a restaurant/coffee shop
...beach to my side

young...
a new hostess has arrived
each time she passes
seating other people
she turns
intentionally catching my glance
she smiles
I smile in return

a new illusion
in the making
a new dream
for the taking

young girl
eyes on me
she winks
when she smiles

who winks
when they smile?

but
she like me
I like her
a perfect life to ruin

there should be something to say
about the situation
there should be a word to describe
life lived in the abyss
but there is not

there should be some way
to describe
the perfect vibration
of the ocean
but there is not
none that I can think of
even though I have existed in it
a million times

there should be something
to stop the brain-break
of the zero
that pounds
in and on
the right side of my skull
but there is not
there is nothing
no one who understands
no way to save me
no way to re-alter this universe

there is nothing

## forty-two

I sit
in a restaurant
that I have gone to
for twenty-five years
I am waited on
by a waitress
that I have known
for twenty of those twenty-five years
she says
*how are you?*
*okay. and you?*
she looks/she thinks/she continues
*you know...*
*I always dug you*
*would you like to take me out?*

all I could do
was to stare into my abstract amazement
smile
with nothing to say

had this been
twenty years ago
I would have taken her up on her offer
for back then
she did cause a few fantasies
to arise
I would have taken her up
I would have broken her heart
like I did to so many others

but this isn't twenty years ago
this is here/this is now

the years have come
and the years have gone
the years have not been so kind to her
as they have been to me
so all I could do
was to look
stare/smile
and remember
what she used to look like
and think
that she should have asked
me that question
then
twenty years ago
then but not now

warm september night
I sit on my patio
a mug of the grape in my hand
the lady
below me
she speaks farsi
into her cell phone
a distant message
in a distant tongue
I look out
to the blackness
the blackness that fills the sky
I look to where
the ocean is supposed to be
but all I see is the blackness
...as farsi rings in my ears
...as I take another sip
from my mug of the grape

I sit/I think/I remember
all this
too much
like the lonely days of summer
summer
many years ago
as I sat
all alone
while others were intertwined
talking about something
saying nothing

back then/me
I was free

didn't have/didn't want to be
no, not with anyone
but freedom
always has a price

now
many years/decades deep
in a relationship
alone
but not alone
it is always this way
the silence
the blackness
in and from the distance
encroaching
coming close/closing in
in the end we are all alone
to think otherwise
is a fool's poison

so a sit here
warm september night
a mug of the grape in my hand
I listen
and I see the
upcoming/oncoming/all-encompassing
blackness

crossing time
love gone by
I see you in the distance

night time shade
visions fade
a glance/a stare
and then you are gone

I walk away

sitin' in the AM
a cup of joe
at my fingertips
I stare out
out across the city
cars/trucks/noise/ugliness
they haunt my world
me
I continue to sit
when I know I should run
me
I've got no where else to be

it the distance
I hear loud hip-hop
the music is approaching
closer and closer
the volumes climbs

soon
entering my vision
a black convertible
maybe ten/fifteen years old
a white guy
with his light brown hair
slicked back
he is at the wheel

his music is blaring
he has those big
boom-boom speakers in his trunk

he pulls up
right in front of where I sit

instead of just pulling
into the parking spot
he swings around
he take/makes
the excess time to back
his car into the spot
…what a loser

I look at him
I look at it/the situation
I laugh in my mind
this is/he draws his influence
directly from
vanilla ice
*ice ice baby* floats in my brain
again, I re-laugh
my brain is amused
this is not 1990
this is 2013

three older ladies
they walk by
*that guy really wants people to look at him*
*doesn't he*
so one questions
again, my mind smiles

the guy who has now fully
backed into the spot
he turns his engine off
he opens his door
he gets out of his ride
cigarette in his hand

he takes a puff
lays the remainder of it
precisely on the side of his car

he looks around
to see who is looking at him

I smile out loud

he goes in the establishment
I continue to sit
stare out
into the abyss of my life/in the city
a few moments later
he reemerges
a bag in his hand
he walks to his car
picks up his still burning cigarette
takes a hit/climbs back inside
starts it up
his music again begins to blare
he thankful drives off

again I am left to the meaningless
silence of the pounding city
with no vision worth looking at
nothing worth seeing
simply a cup of the joe
at my fingertips
I take a sip...

first of all
I am none of those things
that you think I am
none of those shapes
that your mind
has contrived
none of those labels
that you want to place on me

me
who
am
I

a lust live-er
of a dream living
...all of those things
that you wish you could be
if only you could
leave it all behind
but you can't
for it is hard

out here on the outskirts
living the dream is never easy
but once you have crossed the state line
there is no going back

acceptance
most seek acceptance
I do not

redemption
most want redemption
I do not

I choose the lost
the lust for living
the no way in/to the no way out
no way home/to the way it used to be

me, I'm a heretic
I don't care
I don't want your salvation
I don't want your belief
I don't want your reverence
I don't want your promises

for out here on the outskirts
the only knowledge
is self-realized
the only understanding
is what is actually known
not simply believed

belief is for the fool
who wants the promise(s)
of forever/immortality
it doesn't exist

it is/this is/the moment is
in this simply timeframe
all that is – is
then it is gone

this is life
this is knowledge
this is the essence
this is realization
this is me

mistake
by choice

mistake
the ultimate decision

why did I do it?
why didn't I do it?
why didn't I walk the other way?

mistake
the absolute devastation
or the absolute realization

questions
are all that is left

answers
are your decision

mistakes
by choice or by action

mistakes
by decision or karma

mistake
what are you going to make of it

my refrigerator died
bought it NEW ten years ago
it's the first refrigerator
that every passed-away on me

hell, once when I was moving
10+ years ago
I gave my friend who
makes/fixes my guitars
a refrigerator I no longer needed
he put it in the back of his shop
it is still running strong
that mutha fucker must be pushing twenty

my refrigerator died
I did what every good dude would do
I pulled it from the wall
looked at its workings
looked/saw
realized/nothing I could fix
but what I did notice
was that there were a bunch
of those circular plastic top-sealers
the ones that hold water/orange juice
bottle tops in their place

this/that
it made me very sad
they were one of the favorite toys
of the second
of my first batch of persian cats

then/way back when
pushing twenty-five years ago now
I bough my sweet young lady
(she was very young back then)
a little white persian kitten
it/she reminded her
of her favorite cat
a cat that her mother had run over

sad
that kind of shit
always make me sad
I always try to fix
everybody's everything

anyway
paid major dollars
got her that kitten
but that cat got lonely
she
her and I
my babe at the university back then
me
gone A LOT living the acting game
so
we were shopping
when we saw him
a perfect friend/mate
for the other one/the white one
an all black persian
with big copper eyes
yin and yang

I paid major bank for him too
but he was worth every cent
very smart
he loved to play fetch
whenever he wanted to play
he would go and get one of those
circular/plastic bottle-tops
drop it right in front of her/me

maybe eight years ago
he passed on
devastated
didn't cry when my father died
back when I was ten
didn't care when my mother died
back when I was thirty-nine
when he died
it was armageddon
the end
like jim morrision sang with the doors
*this is the end*
ballet for a funeral

but here I sit
all these years later
my refrigerator died
I pulled it out to try and fix it
like life
when it is time to go
it is time to go
but I could/cannot save it/or him
sadly
I did find his favorite toys

his plastic/circle bottle-sealers
they had hidden under the refrigerator
probably knocked there in the play
by the best cat ever
slid there when life was happy
placed there when life still held
fulfillment/hope

now
my refrigerator is broken
and all I am left with
is the sadness of a memory
too painful to every forget
of the perfect friend
that is no longer here

## forty-nine

I walk past
a pair of these cute little hotties
they are standing close to each other
deciding their next step in life
I walk past
thinking/wondering wonderment
a question of possibility
in the abstract flow of life

I walk past but I realize they stink
smell of one/two
too many cigarettes

do smokers not understand
how bad cigarettes make them smell
that scent
lingers/traps/locks
onto a person's person
it stinks

who wants to be with a person like that

people really need to think
before they drink
pondering what they're doing and why

if it doesn't equal enlightenment
if it doesn't walk you down the road
of the holy
then there is no point in doing it

invited to a birthday party
a birthday party in a park
I usually don't go
to weddings/funerals/birthday parties
but it was a family *thAng*
you know...

get to the park
junkyard park
on the southside
of the bad side of a nice city
whatever...

first thing I see is an old man
old man sitting by the sidelines
a crack pipe in his hand

next
I see a weird conglomeration
of a crew walking up to him
head banger/gang banger
& an eleven or twelve year old
all walking hand-in-hand
well, not actually hand-in-hand
but together

they congregate around the old crack head
why
I do not know

the day cruised on
the birthday party moved on

we were fed kfc
shit food for a
waste of life shit day

then came the birthday cake
and the birthday song

me, I passed on the cake
I always do
and I didn't sing along

the party was
what they party was
a young boy turning ten
family/friends
all the meaningless bullshit
that I could never relate to
that goes along with that grouping

kids swung on the swings
climbed on the jungle jim
adults talked
about the things adults talk about

me, I was much more interested
in the sidelines

a old man/crack head
who rode a bike
probably spent all his money
on drugs
couldn't afford a car

old
and cracked out
yet the youth congregated to/around him
white/latin/black
he was the center

the youth would walk off
smoke a joint
same passed out/slept for awhile
others shot hoop
spray painted the walls
when no one was looking
no one
but me

the day went on
the time ticked on
one boy
another year older
the rest of us
just watching life pass by

they
the park dwellers
unusual for l.a.
mix and match
rarely are these groups
seen together
head bangers/gang bangers
black/white/latin

the party
a boring waste of life-time
the cultural surrounding
an interesting observation

that continues to leave my mind
questioning...

why
in a world of why not

sitting
in the fading sun
sitting
in fading life
now
I am old

sitting
at a place
I have sat at
so many-many-many times before
...before
but not now

it has been years
yes, years-years-years
this place
a few miles deep
inland

yet the breeze
from the ocean
always seems to blow here

here/not there

here
where I sit
where I have sat
so many-many-many times before
then/not now

now
I sit
in a different world
life
it has all changed

when did I first start sitting here?
I must have been
twenty-two when this place first opened
twenty-two
that was a long-long-long time ago

I sat here
I loved here
I sat here with a girl I loved

I found another girl here to love
I left the girl I previously loved here
I brought new/different loves with me
here
here where I sit
here
where I have sat
so many-many-many times before

then/not now

now
I am all alone
as I sit here

alone
old

I drink a latte'
a latte'
like I have drank
so many-many-many times before

drink
sit here

I sit
I drink my latte'
I watch
as the young lovers walk
hand-in-hand

hand-in-hand and in love
what a great place to be

young and in love
I remember it well
but it/that was a long-long-long time ago

then/not now

now
I sit here alone

alone
but I guess I'm not really alone
no, not really
I just choose to sit here alone

me, I have this babe

babe
main and central to the cause
a babe
but she hates me
can't blame her
I have done her wrong
a lot of wrong(s)
I've taken many a wrong turn
in the windy road of our relationship

women on the side
women front and center
women here/women there
drinking way too much
way too many times
this and that
but and whatever...
she has stayed
stayed though I didn't want her to
stayed though I wanted a way out
out
to another dream

dream(s)
that's all I live for
a dream fulfilled
is a lie defeated

but ultimately
my advice
advice to everyone

find someone
who will forgive you
forgive you for being who you are
forgive you

and stand by you
no matter what

find that/one of them
it is not easy
but that is my advice

but now/today
she is off
off somewhere else
off to somewhere
doing something
some-thing not no-thing
no, not like me
me
I sit here
with the ocean wind to my back
a cup of the latte'
in front of me
as I sit
as I watch
as I remember
as I dream
about the way
life used to be
when I was young
when I had hope
when I believed

now
I have nothing
nothing but the predestine/predecided alone
as the breeze blows
and I drink my latte'

Scott Shaw is a prolific author, poet, actor, composer, photographer, and filmmaker. Shaw was born and spent his formative years in Hollywood, California and has since spent years of his life living in various geographical locations throughout Asia. His poetry and literary fiction were first published in literary journals in the late 1970s. He continued forward to have several works of poetry and literature published, in book form, beginning in the 1980s. In the later 1980s, due to his extensive documentation of Asian culture, in words and on film, his writings on Anthropology and Asian Studied began to be published, as well. As the 1990s dawned, Shaw's writings began to be embraced in Spiritual and Martial Art circles. From this, he has authored numerous books on Zen Buddhism, Yoga, and the Martial Arts, published by large publishing houses.

## Scott Shaw Books-in-Print include

*About Peace: A 108 Ways to Be At Peace*
*When Things Are Out of Control*
*Advanced Taekwondo*
*Arc Left from Istanbul*
*Bangkok and the Nights of Drunken Stupor*
*Bangkok: Beyond the Buddha*
*Bus Ride(s)*
*Cairo: Before the Aftermath*
*Cambodian Refugees in Long Beach, California:*
*The Definitive Study*
*Chi Kung For Beginners*
*China Deep*
*Echoes from Hell*
*Essence: The Zen of Everything*
*e.q.*
*Hapkido: Articles on Self-Defense*
*Hapkido: Essays on Self-Defense*
*Hapkido: The Korean Art of Self-Defense*
*Hong Kong: Out of Focus*
*Independent Filmmaking: Secrets of the Craft*
*In the Foreboding Shadows of Holiness*
*Israel in the Oblique*
*Junk: The Backstreets of Bangkok*
*Last Will and Testament According to the*
*Divine Rites of the Drug Cocaine*
*L.A.: Tales from the Suburban Side of Hell*
*Los Angeles Skidrow: 1983*
*Marguerite Duras and Charles Bukowski:*
*The Yin and Yang of Modern Erotic Literature*
*Mastering Health: The A to Z of Chi Kung*
*Nirvana in a Nutshell*
*On the Hard Edge of Hollywood*
*Pagan, Burma: Shadows of the Stupa*

*Sake' in a Glass, Sushi with Your Fingers:*
*Fifteen Minutes in Tokyo*
*Scream: Southeast Asia and the Dream*
*Samurai Zen*
*Sedona: Realm of the Vortex*
*Shama Baba*
*Shanghai Whispers Shanghai Screams*
*Shattered Thoughts*
*Singaore: Off Center*
*South Korea in a Blur*
*Suicide Slowly*
*Taekwondo Basics*
*Ten to Thirty*
*The Ki Process:*
*Korean Secrets for Cultivating Dynamic Energy*
*The Little Book of Yoga Breathing*
*The Little Book of Zen Mediation*
*The Most Beautiful Woman in Shanghai*
*The Passionate Kiss of Illusion*
*The Screenplays*
*The Tao of Chi*
*The Tao of Self Defense*
*The Voodoo Buddha*
*The Warrior is Silent:*
*Martial Arts and the Spiritual Path*
*The Zen of Modern Life and the Reality of Reality*
*TKO: Lost Nights in Tokyo*
*Wet Dreams and Placid Silence*
*Yoga: A Spiritual Guidebook*
*Yosemite: End of the Winter*
*Zen Buddhism: The Pathway to Nirvana*
*Zen Filmmaking*
*Zen in the Blink of an Eye*
*Zen O'clock: Time to Be*
*Zen: Tales from the Journey*
*Zero One*

www.ingramcontent.com/pod-product-compliance
Lightning Source LLC
Chambersburg PA
CBHW060358090426
42734CB00011B/2177